Thoughts on

OPPORTUNITY

TRIUMPH BOOKS
CHICAGO

This edition is published by Triumph Books, Chicago,
by arrangement with Forbes Inc.

Library of Congress Cataloging in Publication Data

Thoughts on opportunity.
    p. cm. — (The Forbes Leadership Library)
Includes index.
ISBN 1-57243-279-9 (hardcover)
1. Success—Quotations, maxims, etc.   2. Conduct of life—
Quotations, maxims, etc.   I. Series.
PN6084.S78T457   1998
646.7—dc21   98-18084
                                                              CIP

This book is available in quantity at special discounts
for your group or organization. For more information, contact:

TRIUMPH BOOKS
644 South Clark Street
Chicago, Illinois 60605
(312) 939-3330 FAX (312) 663-3557

Book design by Graffolio.
Cover design © 1998 by Triumph Books.
Illustrations from the Dover Pictorial Archive Series
used with permission.
Some of the properties in the photograph on the front cover
courtesy of Marshall Field's Corporate Gifts and Incentives.

Printed in the United States of America

CONTENTS

INTRODUCTION

The moving motive in establishing FORBES Magazine, in 1917, was ardent desire to promulgate humaneness in business, then woefully lacking. . . .

Every issue of FORBES, since its inception, has appeared under the masthead: "With all thy getting, get understanding."

Not only so, but we have devoted, all through the years, a full page to "Thoughts on the Business of Life," reflections by ancient and modern sages calculated to inspire a philosophic mode of life, broad sympathies, charity towards all. . . .

I have faith that the time will eventually come when employees and employers, as well as all mankind, will realize that they serve themselves best when they serve others most.

B. C. Forbes

ABILITY

As tools become rusty,
so does the mind;
a garden uncared for
soon becomes smothered in weeds;
a talent neglected
withers and dies.

ETHEL PAGE

The real tragedy of life
is not in being limited to one talent,
but in the failure
to use the one talent.

EDGAR WORK

English history is aristocracy
with the doors open.
Who has courage and faculty,
let him come in.

RALPH WALDO EMERSON

———

I believe that God felt sorry for actors
so he created Hollywood
to give them a place in the sun
and a swimming pool.
The price they had to pay
was to surrender their talent.

SIR CEDRIC HARDWICKE

———

So much one man can do
that does both act and know.

ANDREW MARVELL

The tools to him
who has the ability
to handle them.

FRENCH PROVERB

The richest soil,
if uncultivated,
produces the rankest weeds.

PLUTARCH

I think most of the people
involved in any art
always secretly wonder
whether they are there
because they're good
or there because they're lucky.

KATHARINE HEPBURN

Ability has nothing to do
with opportunity.

NAPOLEON BONAPARTE

———

Use a sweet tongue,
courtesy, and gentleness,
and thou mayst manage
to guide an elephant with a hair.

SAADI

———

Ability will never catch up
with the demand for it.

MALCOLM FORBES

Trust also your own judgement,
for it is your most reliable counselor.
A man's mind
has sometimes a way of telling him
more than seven watchmen
posted on a high tower.

ECCLESIASTICUS

ACHIEVEMENT

Diligence,
as it avails in all things,
is also of the utmost movement
in pleading causes.
Diligence is to be
particularly cultivated by us;
it is to be constantly exerted;
it is capable of effecting
almost everything.

CICERO

Things are pretty, graceful,
rich, elegant, handsome,
but until they speak
to the imagination,
not yet beautiful.

RALPH WALDO EMERSON

If there were in the world today
any large number of people
who desired their own happiness
more than they desired
the unhappiness of others,
we could have a paradise
in a few years.

BERTRAND RUSSELL

Treat people as if they were
what they ought to be
and you help them become
what they are capable of becoming.

JOHANN WOLFGANG VON GOETHE

Virtue, as such,
naturally procures
considerable advantages
to the virtuous.

JOSEPH BUTLER

———❖———

Gullibility
is the key to all adventures.
The greenhorn is the ultimate victor
in everything;
it is he that gets
the most out of life.

GILBERT K. CHESTERTON

Whatever your grade or position,
if you know how and when to speak,
and when to remain silent,
your chances of real success
are proportionately increased.

RALPH C. SMEDLEY

The best place to succeed
is where you are
with what you have.

CHARLES M. SCHWAB

The awareness of the ambiguity
of one's highest achievements
(as well as one's deepest failures)
is a definite symptom
of maturity.

PAUL TILLICH

Nothing is unthinkable,
nothing impossible
to the balanced person,
provided it comes out of the needs of life
and is dedicated
to life's further developments.

LEWIS MUMFORD

We are each of us angels
with only one wing,
and we can only fly
by embracing each other.

LUCIANO DE CRESCENZO

The chief obstacle
to the progress of the human race
is the human race.

DON MARQUIS

The cloak of naïveté
was the uniform of our success:
we didn't know
it couldn't be done.

MARK PETERS

To travel hopefully
is a better thing than to arrive,
and the true success
is to labor.

ROBERT LOUIS STEVENSON

Always the path
of American destiny
has been into the unknown.
Always there arose
enough reserves of strength,
balances of sanity,
portions of wisdom
to carry the nation
through to a fresh start
with ever-renewing vitality.

CARL SANDBURG

———

The three grand essentials
of happiness are:
something to do,
someone to love,
and something to hope for.

ALEXANDER CHALMERS

Praise is well,
compliment is well,
but affection—
that is the last
and most precious reward
that any man can win,
whether by character
or achievement.

MARK TWAIN

———

There is only one way
to happiness,
and that is cease worrying about things
which are beyond the power
of our will.

EPICTETUS

Make no little plans:
They have no magic
to stir men's blood.

DANIEL H. BURNHAM

True, you can't take it with you,
but then, that's not the place
where it comes in handy.

BRENDAN FRANCIS

ACTION

Begin doing
what you want to do now.
We are not living in eternity.
We have only this moment,
sparkling like a star in our hand—
and melting like a snowflake.
Let us use it before it is too late.

MARIE BEYNON RAY

Respectable men and women
content with the good and easy living
are missing some of the most important things in life.
Unless you give yourself
to some great cause
you haven't even begun to live.

WILLIAM MERRILL

Know the true value of time;
snatch, seize, and enjoy
every moment of it.
No idleness, no laziness
or procrastination.

LORD CHESTERFIELD

So act
that your principle of action
might safely be made
a law for the whole world.

IMMANUEL KANT

Nothing will ever be attempted,
if all possible objections
must first be overcome.

SAMUEL JOHNSON

Unless there be correct thought,
there cannot be correct action,
and when there is correct thought,
right action will follow.

HENRY GEORGE

Activity makes more men's fortunes
than cautiousness.

MARQUIS DE VAUVENARGUES

I shall tell you a great secret, my friend.
Do not wait for the last judgement,
it takes place every day.

ALBERT CAMUS

The basic test of freedom
is perhaps less
in what we are free to do
than in what we are free
not to do.

ERIC HOFFER

—◆—

No minute lost
Comes ever back again.
Take heed and see
Ye nothing do in vain.

LONDON CLOCK TOWER MOTTO

—◆—

There's a better way
to do it.
Find it!

THOMAS A. EDISON

I expect to pass through life
but once.
If, therefore,
there can be any kindness
I can show,
or any good thing
I can do to any fellow being,
let me do it now
and not defer or neglect it,
as I shall not pass
this way again.

WILLIAM PENN

Don't think
of how you're going to spend your time—
use it.

WILMA ASKINAS

Leadership is action,
not position.

DONALD H. MCGANNON

The world is moving so fast
these days
that the man who says it can't be done
is generally interrupted by someone
doing it.

ELBERT HUBBARD

We are all, it seems,
saving ourselves
for the senior prom.
But many of us forget
that somewhere along the way
we must learn to dance.

ALAN HARRINGTON

ATTITUDE

To be seeing the world
made new every morning,
as if it were the morning
of the first day,
and then to make the most of it
for the individual soul
as if each were the last day—
is the daily curriculum
of the mind's desire.

JOHN H. FINLEY

The only limit
to our realization of tomorrow
will be our doubts
of today.

FRANKLIN D. ROOSEVELT

It is a sad thing
to begin life
with low conceptions of it.
It may not be possible
for a young man to measure life;
but it is possible to say,
I am resolved to put life
to its noblest and best use.

THEODORE T. MUNGER

Enthusiasm
is the greatest asset in the world.
It beats money and power
and influence.
It is no more or less
than faith in action.

HENRY CHESTER

The world is as large
as the range of one's interests.
A narrow-minded man
has a narrow outlook.
The walls of his world
shut out the broader horizon
of affairs.
Prejudice can maintain walls
that no invention can remove.

JOSEPH JASTROW

The man who is cocksure
that he has arrived
is ready for the return journey.

B. C. FORBES

It is our attitude
toward events,
not events themselves,
which we can control.
Nothing is by its own nature calamitous—
even death is terrible
only if we fear it.

EPICTETUS

One of the illusions of life
is that the present hour
is not the critical, decisive hour.
Write it on your heart
that every day
is the best day of the year.

RALPH WALDO EMERSON

I feel the responsibility
of the occasion.
Responsibility is proportionate
to opportunity.

WOODROW WILSON

Most of us
spend our lives
as if we had another one
in the bank.

BEN IRWIN

Angels fly
because they take themselves
lightly.

GILBERT K. CHESTERTON

CHARACTER

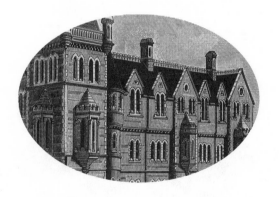

I do not mean to expose my ideas
to ingenious ridicule
by maintaining that everything happens
to every man for the best;
but I will contend,
that he who makes the best use of it
fulfills that part
of a wise and good man.

RICHARD CUMBERLAND

Faced with crisis,
the man of character
falls back on himself.

CHARLES DE GAULLE

Every man's work,
whether it be literature
or music or pictures
or anything else,
is always a portrait
of himself,
and the more he tries
to conceal himself
the more clearly
will his character appear
in spite of himself.

SAMUEL BUTLER

No man is free
who is not master
of himself.

EPICTETUS

No man
knows his true character
until he has run out of gas,
purchased something
on the installment plan
and raised an adolescent.

MERCELENE COX

It is within the power
of every man
to live his life nobly,
but of no man to live forever.
Yet so many of us hope
that life will go on forever,
and so few aspire to live nobly.

SENECA

Only a person
who has faith in himself
can be faithful to others.

ERICH FROMM

How you react
when the joke's on you
can reveal your character.

ROBERT HALF

It is in trifles,
and when he is off his guard,
that a man
best shows his character.

ARTHUR SCHOPENHAUER

Let us endeavor so to live
that when we come to die
even the undertaker will be sorry.

MARK TWAIN

The measure of a man's real character
is what he would do
if he knew
he would never be found out.

THOMAS B. MACAULAY

No great man
ever complains
of want of opportunity.

RALPH WALDO EMERSON

CREATIVITY

Creative thinking
is today's most prized,
profit-producing possession
for any individual, corporation,
or country.
It has the capacity
to change you,
your business,
and the world.

ROBERT CRAWFORD

Most ideas
are step-by-step children
of other ideas.

ALEX OSBORN

The creative person
is both more primitive
and more cultivated,
more destructive and more constructive,
a lot madder and a lot saner,
than the average person.

DR. FRANK BARRON

———

The rewards in business
go to the man
who does something
with an idea.

WILLIAM BENTON

———

Imagination
is more important
than knowledge.

ALBERT EINSTEIN

Discoveries
are often made
by not following instructions;
by going off the main roads;
by trying the untried.

FRANK TYGER

No man
ever made a great discovery
without the exercise
of the imagination.

GEORGE HENRY LEWIS

The less of routine,
the more of life.

AMOS BRONSON ALCOTT

———

Let a salad-maker
be a spendthrift for oil,
a miser for vinegar,
a statesman for salt,
and a madman for mixing.

SPANISH PROVERB

———

I don't know
if Bacon wrote the works of Shakespeare,
but if he did not,
he missed the opportunity
of his life.

JAMES M. BARRIE

We bury the men
who do the nation's creative work
under layers of administrators
and mountains of memoranda.
We shrivel creativity
by endless frustrations.

ADMIRAL H. G. RICKOVER

If you turn the imagination loose
like a hunting dog,
it will often return
with the bird in its mouth.

WILLIAM MAXWELL

Money never starts an idea;
it is the idea
that starts the money.

W. J. CAMERON

DIFFICULTY

A certain amount
of opposition
is a great help to a man;
it is what he wants
and must have
to be good for anything.
Hardship and opposition
are the native soil
of manhood and self-reliance.

JOHN NEAL

Self-pity
is our worst enemy,
and if we yield to it,
we can never do anything wise
in the world.

HELEN KELLER

To be thrown upon
one's own resources
is to be cast into the very lap
of fortune;
for our faculties then undergo
a development
and display an energy
of which they were previously
unsusceptible.

BENJAMIN FRANKLIN

Failure is success
if we learn from it.

MALCOLM FORBES

Beside the practical knowledge
which defeat offers,
there are important personality profits
to be taken.
Defeat strips away false values
and makes you realize
what you really want.
It stops you from chasing butterflies
and puts you to work digging gold.

WILLIAM MARSTON

Mistakes
are part of the dues one pays
for a full life.

SOPHIA LOREN

Poverty is very terrible,
and sometimes kills
the very soul within us;
but it is the north wind
that lashes men into Vikings;
it is the soft, luscious south wind
which lulls them to lotus dreams.

OUIDA

Difficulties exist
to be surmounted.

RALPH WALDO EMERSON

A man's greatest enemies
are his own apathy
and stubbornness.

FRANK TYGER

Don't be discouraged
by a failure.
It can be a positive experience.
Failure is,
in a sense,
the highway to success,
inasmuch as every discovery of what is false
leads us to seek earnestly
after what is true,
and every fresh experience points out
some form of error
which we shall afterwards
carefully avoid.

JOHN KEATS

There is the greatest practical benefit
in making a few failures
early in life.

THOMAS HUXLEY

One must be thrust out
of a finished cycle in life,
and that leap
is the most difficult to make—
to part with one's faith, one's love,
when one would prefer
to renew the faith
and recreate the passion.

ANAIS NIN

There is in
the worst of fortune
the best of chances
for a happy change.

EURIPIDES

A smooth sea
never made a skilled mariner.

ENGLISH PROVERB

We learn from our mistakes,
and the amount we learn
is in direct proportion
to the amount we suffer
from having made the mistakes.

FOOTBALL COACH TOMMY PROTHRO

Adversity
introduces a man to himself.

ANONYMOUS

Our greatest glory
consists not in never failing,
but in rising every time we fall.

OLIVER GOLDSMITH

DISCOVERY

It is happily and kindly provided
that in every life
there are certain pauses,
and interruptions which force consideration
upon the careless,
and seriousness upon the light;
points of time
where one course of action ends
and another begins.

SAMUEL JOHNSON

There is no security
on this earth.
Only opportunity.

DOUGLAS MACARTHUR

To him who looks
upon the world rationally,
the world in its turn
presents a rational aspect.
The relation is mutual.

GEORG WILHELM HEGEL

Life is a magic vase
filled to the brim;
so made that you cannot dip into it
nor draw from it;
but it overflows into the hand
that drops treasures into it—
drop in malice
and it overflows hate;
drop in charity
and it overflows love.

JOHN RUSKIN

A man that does not know
how to be angry
does not know
how to be good.

HENRY WARD BEECHER

The universe is full
of magical things,
patiently waiting for our wits
to grow sharper.

EDEN PHILPOTTS

Summer ends,
and autumn comes,
and he who would have it otherwise
would have high tide always
and a full moon every night.

HAL BORLAND

The light that a man receiveth
by counsel from another
is drier and purer than that which cometh
from his own understanding and judgement,
which is ever infused and drenched
in his affections and customs.

FRANCIS BACON

The more we study,
the more we discover our ignorance.

PERCY BYSSHE SHELLEY

We are generally better persuaded
by the reasons we discover ourselves
than by those given to us by others.

BLAISE PASCAL

———✦———

Life is half spent
before one knows what it is.

FRENCH PROVERB

———✦———

The art of being wise
is knowing what to overlook.

WILLIAM JAMES

———✦———

A loving heart
is the beginning
of all knowledge.

THOMAS CARLYLE

If we could be twice young
and twice old
we could correct
all our mistakes.

EURIPIDES

I remember my youth
and the feeling
that will never come back any more—
the feeling that I could last forever,
outlast the sea,
the earth, and all men.

JOSEPH CONRAD

Life has not taught me
to expect nothing,
but she has taught me
not to expect success
to be the inevitable result
of my endeavors.

ALAN PATON

———

Wisdom outweighs
any wealth.

SOPHOCLES

———

Men occasionally stumble
over the truth,
but most of them pick themselves up
and hurry off
as if nothing had happened.

WINSTON CHURCHILL

DREAMS

All ambitions are lawful
except those which climb upward
on the miseries or credulities
of mankind.

JOSEPH CONRAD

More tears are shed
over answered prayers
than unanswered ones.

ST. THERESA OF AVILA

If I keep a green bough
in my heart,
the singing bird will come.

CHINESE PROVERB

Make yourselves nests
of pleasant thoughts.
None of us knows
what fairy palaces we may build
of beautiful thought—
proof against all adversity.
Bright fancies,
satisfied memories,
noble histories,
faithful sayings,
treasure houses
of precious and restful thoughts,
which care cannot disturb,
nor pain make gloomy,
nor poverty
take away from us.

JOHN RUSKIN

Illusion
is always based on reality,
for its strength depends
upon its fit with the desires,
fears and experiences
of countless humans.

JOHN P. GRIER

Our aspirations
are our possibilities.

ROBERT BROWNING

You see things;
and you say "Why?"
But I dream things
that never were;
and I say "Why not?"

GEORGE BERNARD SHAW

When you cease to dream
you cease to live.

MALCOLM FORBES

———⊶⊷———

True hope is swift,
and flies with swallow's wings.
Kings it makes gods,
and meaner creatures kings.

WILLIAM SHAKESPEARE

———⊶⊷———

We must select the illusion
which appeals to our temperament,
and embrace it with passion,
if we want to be happy.

CYRIL CONNOLLY

It appears to me
that almost any man may,
like the spider,
spin from his own
inwards his own airy citadel.

JOHN KEATS

We do not really feel grateful
toward those who make
our dreams come true;
they ruin our dreams.

ERIC HOFFER

EDUCATION

He who calls
in the aid of equal understanding
doubles his own;
and he who profits
of a superior understanding
raises his powers to a level
with the height
of the superior understanding
he unites with.

EDMUND BURKE

The mind
is but barren soil;
a soil which is soon exhausted,
and will produce no crop,
or only one,
unless it be continually fertilized
and enriched
with foreign matter.

JOSHUA REYNOLDS

Each new development
starts from something else.
It does not come out of a blue sky.
You make real use of that
which has already entered the mind . . .
That is the real reason
for accumulating knowledge.

ROBERT CRAWFORD

Reading
makes a full man,
meditation
a profound man,
discourse
a clear man.

BENJAMIN FRANKLIN

Children have to be educated,
but they also have to be left
to educate themselves.

ERNEST DIMNET

My education began
with a set of blocks
which had on them
the Roman numerals
and the letters of the alphabet.
It is not yet finished.

CALVIN COOLIDGE

That which we do not call education
is more precious
than that which we call so.

RALPH WALDO EMERSON

Whoso neglects learning
in his youth
loses the past
and is dead for the future.

EURIPIDES

A child's education should begin
at least 100 years
before he was born.

OLIVER WENDELL HOLMES

They know enough
who know how to learn.

HENRY ADAMS

The most valuable result
of all education
is to make you do the thing
you have to do,
when it ought to be done,
whether you like it or not.

THOMAS HUXLEY

———

The direction
in which education starts a man
will determine his future life.

PLATO

———

We have an infinite amount to learn
both from nature
and each other.

JOHN GLENN

Knowledge without wisdom
is a load of books
on the back of an ass.

JAPANESE PROVERB

In the final analysis
it is not what you do
for your children
but what you have taught them to do
for themselves
that will make them
successful human beings.

ANN LANDERS

Knowledge
is a comfortable and necessary
retreat and shelter for us
in an advanced age;
and if we do not plant it
while young,
it will give us no shade
when we grow old.

LORD CHESTERFIELD

Education makes a greater difference
between man and man
than nature has made
between man and brute.

JOHN ADAMS

EXPERIENCE

No man
was ever so completely skilled
in the conduct of life,
as not to receive new information
from age and experience.

TERENCE

Events
are only the shells of ideas;
and often it is the fluent thought of ages
that is crystallized in a moment
by the stroke of a pen
or the point of a bayonet.

EDWIN CHAPIN

Have no fear
of change as such and,
on the other hand,
no liking for it
merely for its own sake.

ROBERT MOSES

———⊷•⊶———

It is when we all play safe
that we create a world
of utmost insecurity.

DAG HAMMARSKJÖLD

———⊷•⊶———

There are only two or three
human stories,
and they go on
repeating themselves
as fiercely as if
they had never happened before.

WILLA CATHER

The trouble with experience
is that by the time you have it
you are too old to take advantage of it.

JIMMY CONNORS

The brevity of human life
gives a melancholy
to the profession
of the architect.

RALPH WALDO EMERSON

You will always find
some Eskimos
willing to instruct the Congolese
on how to cope with heat waves.

STANISLAUS LEC

Experience is not
what happens to a man,
it is what a man does
with what happens to him.

ALDOUS HUXLEY

Life is the greatest bargain:
We get it for nothing.

YIDDISH PROVERB

Whoever has lived long enough
to find out what life is,
knows how deep a debt of gratitude
we owe to Adam,
the first great benefactor
of our race.
He brought death
into the world.

MARK TWAIN

Life is the only art
that we are required to practice
without preparation,
and without being allowed
the preliminary trials,
the failures and botches,
that are essential for training.

LEWIS MUMFORD

Time ripens
all things.
No man's born wise.

MIGUEL DE CERVANTES

I have had enough experience
in all my years,
and have read enough of the past,
to know that advice to grandchildren
is usually wasted.
If the second and third generations
could profit by the experience
of the first generation,
we would not be having
some of the troubles
we have today.

HARRY S. TRUMAN

Experience
is the hardest teacher.
It gives you the test first
and the lesson afterward.

ANONYMOUS

It is good to have an end
to journey towards,
but it is the journey that matters,
in the end.

URSULA LE GUIN

What we know here
is very little,
but what we are ignorant of
is immense.

LAPLACE

Prudence
is but experience,
which equal time
equally bestows on all men,
in all things
they equally apply themselves unto.

THOMAS HOBBES

Live all you can;
it's a mistake not to.
It doesn't so much matter
what you do in particular,
so long as you have your life.
If you haven't had that,
what have you had?

HENRY JAMES

No mistakes,
no experience;
no experience,
no wisdom.

STANLEY GOLDSTEIN

The life of every man
is a diary
in which he means to write one story,
and writes another;
and his humblest hour
is when he compares
the volume as it is
with what he vowed to make of it.

JAMES M. BARRIE

FORESIGHT

Unless a man
has trained himself
for his chance,
the chance will only make him
ridiculous.
A great occasion
is worth to a man
exactly what his antecedents
have enabled him to make of it.

WILLIAM MATTHEWS

There is an ambush everywhere
from the army of accidents;
therefore the rider of life
runs with loosened reins.

HAFIZ

Great opportunities
come to all,
but many do not know
they have met them.
The only preparation
to take advantage of them
is single fidelity to watch
what each day brings.

ALBERT DUNNING

The pace of events
is moving so fast
that unless we can find
some way to keep our sights
on tomorrow,
we cannot expect to be in touch
with today.

DEAN RUSK

Business
more than any other occupation
is a continual dealing
with the future;
it is a continual calculation,
an instinctive exercise
in foresight.

HENRY R. LUCE

———※———

He who does nothing
renders himself incapable
of doing any thing;
but while we are executing any work,
we are preparing
and qualifying ourselves
to undertake another.

WILLIAM HAZLITT

Speak softly and sweetly.
If your words
are soft and sweet,
they won't be as hard to swallow
if you have to eat them.

ANONYMOUS

That men do not learn very much
from the lessons of history
is the most important
of all the lessons
history has to teach.

ALDOUS HUXLEY

The wise man avoids evil
by anticipating it.

PUBLILIUS SYRUS

The first essential character [of civilization],
I should say, is forethought.
This, I would say,
is what distinguishes men from brutes
and adults from children.

BERTRAND RUSSELL

A danger foreseen
is half avoided.

THOMAS FULLER

Only those
who get into scrapes
with their eyes open
can find a safe way out.

LOGAN PEARSALL SMITH

⚬

If you don't know
where you are going,
every road
will get you nowhere.

HENRY KISSINGER

⚬

In every generation
there has to be some fool
who will speak the truth
as he sees it.

BORIS PASTERNAK

Before you kick the dog,
find out the name
of its master.

RAY E. BROWN

In respect to foresight and firmness,
the people are more prudent,
more stable,
and have better judgement
than princes.

NICCOLO MACHIAVELLI

FORTUNE

Remember the Three Princes of Serendip
who went out
looking for treasure?
They didn't find
what they were looking for,
but they kept finding things
just as valuable.
That's serendipity,
and our business [drugs]
is full of it.

GEORGE MERCK

❦

Life is a gamble
at terrible odds;
if it was a bet
you wouldn't take it.

TOM STOPPARD

And think not
you can guide the course of love.
For love,
if it finds you worthy,
shall guide your course.

KAHLIL GIBRAN

Name the greatest
of all inventors.
Accident.

MARK TWAIN

Chance does nothing
that has not been prepared
beforehand.

ALEXIS DE TOCQUEVILLE

We cannot bear
to regard ourselves
simply as playthings
of blind chance;
we cannot admit
to feeling ourselves abandoned.

UGO BETTI

All of life is happenstance,
A maze of drive and hope and chance:
For starters, why were we conceived?
For endings, what's to be believed?

ART BUCK

Failure or success
seem to be allotted to men
by their stars.
But they retain the power of wriggling,
of fighting with their star
or against it,
and in the whole universe
the only really interesting movement
is this wriggle.

E. M. FORSTER

We are not permitted to choose
the frame of our destiny.
But what we put into it
is ours.

DAG HAMMARSKJÖLD

How easy 'tis, when
Destiny proves kind,
With full-spread sails to
run before the wind!

JOHN DRYDEN

Thy lot or portion of life
is seeking after thee;
therefore be at rest from
seeking after it.

ALI IBN-ALI-TALIB

If fortune calls,
offer him a seat.

YIDDISH PROVERB

Man's destiny
lies half within himself,
half without.
To advance in either half
at the expense of the other
is literally insane.

PHILIP WYLIE

Your luck
is how you treat people.

BRIDGET O'DONNELL

If fate means you to lose,
give him a good fight anyhow.

WILLIAM MCFEE

Love nothing
but that which comes to you
woven in the pattern
of your destiny.

MARCUS AURELIUS

FUTURE

Life is divided
into three terms—
that which was, which is,
and which will be.
Let us learn from the past
to profit by the present
and from the present
to live better for the future.

WILLIAM WORDSWORTH

Future:
That period of time
in which our affairs prosper,
our friends are true
and our happiness
is assured.

AMBROSE BIERCE

The future
is a great land;
a man cannot go around it
in a day;
he cannot measure it
with a bound;
he cannot bind its harvests
into a single sheaf.
It is wider than vision,
and has no end.

DONALD G. MITCHELL

You can never plan the future
by the past.

EDMUND BURKE

Everyone's future is,
in reality,
an urn full of unknown treasures
from which all may draw
unguessed prizes.

LORD DUNSANY

❦

I like the dreams of the future
better than the history
of the past.

THOMAS JEFFERSON

❦

They gave each other
a smile with a future in it.

RING LARDNER

My interest
is in the future
because I am going to spend
the rest of my life there.

CHARLES F. KETTERING

Only mothers
can think of the future,
because they give birth to it
in their children.

MAXIM GORKY

The future you shall know
when it has come;
before then,
forget it.

AESCHYLUS

It is a mistake
to look too far ahead.
Only one link
of the chain of destiny
can be handled at a time.

WINSTON CHURCHILL

A nation without dregs
and malcontents
is orderly, peaceful and pleasant,
but perhaps without the seed
of things to come.

ERIC HOFFER

Man will never be entirely willing
to give up this world for the next
nor the next world for this.

WILLIAM INGE

GENIUS

When a true genius
appears in the world
you may know him
by this sign:
that all the dunces
are in confederation
against him.

JONATHAN SWIFT

The notes I handle
no better than many pianists.
But the pauses between the notes—
ah, that is where the art resides.

ARTUR SCHNABEL

A great mind
is one that can forget
or look beyond itself.

WILLIAM HAZLITT

———✦———

Fame
due to the achievements of the mind
never perishes.

PROPERTIUS

———✦———

There is no genius in life
like the genius of energy
and activity.

DONALD G. MITCHELL

Of all the many earthly resources
we have at our command
it is only our minds
and the associated unique processes
that are truly infinite.

CRAIG DAY

He who has learning
without imagination
has feet but no wings.

STANLEY GOLDSTEIN

Genius is perseverance
in disguise.

MIKE NEWLIN

If there were no falsehood in the world,
there would be no doubt;
if there were no doubt,
there would be no inquiry;
if no inquiry, no wisdom,
no knowledge, no genius.

WALTER SAVAGE LANDOR

In art
nothing worth doing
can be done without genius;
in science
even a very moderate capacity
can contribute
to a supreme achievement.

BERTRAND RUSSELL

The principal mark of genius
is not perfection
but originality,
the opening of new frontiers.

ARTHUR KOESTLER

INDUSTRY

Most of life is routine—
dull and grubby,
but routine is the momentum
that keeps a man going.
If you wait for inspiration
you'll be standing on the corner
after the parade
is a mile down the street.

BEN NICHOLAS

Work only
half a day.
It makes no difference
which half—
the first 12 hours
or the last 12 hours.

KEMMONS WILSON

Work spares us
from three great evils:
boredom,
vice
and need.

FRANÇOIS MARIE AROUET VOLTAIRE

One's lifework,
I have learned,
grows with the working
and the living.
Do it as if your life depended on it,
and the first thing you know,
you'll have made a life out of it.

THERESA HELBURN

Blessed is he
who has found his work;
let him ask
no other blessedness.

THOMAS CARLYLE

Work is not a curse;
it is the prerogative of intelligence,
the only means to manhood,
and the measure
of civilization.

CALVIN COOLIDGE

Far and away the best prize
that life offers
is the chance to work hard
at work worth doing.

THEODORE ROOSEVELT

To get profit
without risk,
experience
without danger,
and reward
without work,
is as impossible
as it is to live
without being born.

A. P. GOUTHEV

Backboneless employees
are too ready to attribute
the success of others to "luck."
Luck is usually the fruit
of intelligent application.
The man who is intent
on making the most of his opportunities
is too busy
to bother about luck.

B. C. FORBES

I'm a great believer in luck;
and I find that
the harder I work
the more I have of it.

STEPHEN LEACOCK

God sells us all things
at the price of labor.

LEONARDO DA VINCI

⸺✦⸺

You don't get anything
clean
without getting something else
dirty.

CECIL BAXTER

⸺✦⸺

Work is hard
if you're paid to do it,
and it's pleasure
if you pay
to be allowed to do it.

FINLEY PETER DUNNE

No human pursuit
achieves dignity
unless it can be called work,
and when you can experience
a physical loneliness
for the tools of your trade,
you see that the other things—
the experiments,
the irrelevant vocations,
the vanities you used to hold—
were false to you.

BERYL MARKHAM

The majority prove their worth
by keeping busy.
A busy life is the nearest thing
to a purposeful life.

ERIC HOFFER

Make it a point
to do something every day
that you don't want to do.
This is the golden rule
for acquiring the habit
of doing your duty without pain.

MARK TWAIN

In the ordinary business
of life,
industry can do anything
which genius can do,
and very many things
which it cannot.

HENRY WARD BEECHER

The best fertilizer
is the owner's footprint.

SOUTH CAROLINA SAYING

God will provide the victuals,
but He will not
cook the dinner.

ANONYMOUS

If you want to leave
your footprints
on the sands of time,
be sure you're wearing work shoes.

ITALIAN PROVERB

INITIATIVE

Someone has said
that the "p" is silent
in the word "luck,"
but it belongs there nevertheless.
Investigation usually turns up the fact
that the lucky fellow
is the plucky fellow
who has been burning midnight oil
and taking defeat after defeat
with a smile.

JAMES HILL

The meek shall inherit the earth,
but not the mineral rights.

J. PAUL GETTY

Neither a wise man
nor a brave man
lies down on the tracks of history
to wait for the train of the future
to run over him.

DWIGHT D. EISENHOWER

To do anything in this world
worth doing,
we must not stand back shivering
and thinking of the cold and danger,
but jump in,
and scramble through
as well as we can.

SYDNEY SMITH

Act quickly,
think slowly.

GREEK PROVERB

The method of the enterprising
is to plan with audacity
and execute with vigor.

CHRISTIAN BOVEE

It's them as take advantage
that get advantage i' this world.

GEORGE ELIOT

I don't wait for moods.
You accomplish nothing
if you do that.
Your mind must know
it has got to get down to earth.

PEARL BUCK

I can think of few
important movements for reform
in which success was won
by any method
other than an energetic minority
presenting the indifferent majority
with a fait accompli,
which was then accepted.

VERA BRITTAIN

It's a terrible shame
if you're born
the brightest guy in your class.
If you're not,
then you have to hustle—
and that's good.

HAL PRINCE

If you don't know
what you want to do,
it's harder to do it.

MALCOLM FORBES

He that would have fruit
must climb the tree.

THOMAS FULLER

PERCEPTION

In every object
there is inexhaustible meaning;
the eye sees in it
what the eye brings means
of seeing.

THOMAS CARLYLE

Fear not
that thy life
shall come to an end,
but rather fear
that it shall never have
a beginning.

JOHN HENRY NEWMAN

If we think of life as a journey
and consider it to be the opportunity
for getting from where we are
to where we want to be,
we will have a working rule
that provides us with both a purpose
and expanding possibilities for our lives.

FRED P. CORSON

———◦◦◦———

We don't see things
as they are,
we see things
as we are.

ANAIS NIN

———◦◦◦———

I should like to enjoy this summer
flower by flower,
as if it were to be the last for me.

ANDRÉ GIDE

How sad would be November
if we had no knowledge
of the spring!

EDWIN TEALE

It's hard to see a halo
when you're looking for horns.

CULLEN HIGHTOWER

Only in a quiet mind
is adequate perception
of the world.

HANS MARGOLIUS

One should . . .
be able to see things as hopeless
and yet be determined
to make them otherwise.

F. SCOTT FITZGERALD

To young people,
everything looks permanent,
established—
and in their eyes
everything should be,
needs to be changed.
To older people
everything seems to change,
and in their view
almost nothing should.

MALCOLM FORBES

When one door closes
another door opens;
but we often look so long
and so regretfully
upon the closed door
that we do not see
the ones which open
for us.

ALEXANDER GRAHAM BELL

Bad times, hard times—
this is what people keep saying;
but let us live well,
and times shall be good.
We are the times:
Such as we are,
such are the times.

ST. AUGUSTINE

Mistakes
are a fact of life:
It is the response to the error
that counts.

NIKKI GIOVANNI

———

The greatest blunders,
like the thickest ropes,
are often compounded
of a multitude of strands.
Take the rope apart,
separate it into the small strands that compose it,
and you can break them
one by one. You think,
"That is all there was!"
But twist them all together
and you have something tremendous.

VICTOR HUGO

Beware
lest you lose the substance
by grasping at the shadow.

AESOP

——◆◆◆——

An adventure
is only an inconvenience
rightly considered.
An inconvenience
is only an adventure
wrongly considered.

GILBERT K. CHESTERTON

VISION

So many new ideas
are at first strange and horrible
though ultimately valuable
that a very heavy responsibility
rests upon those
who would prevent
their dissemination.

JOHN B. S. HALDANE

You cannot speak of ocean
to a well-frog,
the creature of a narrower sphere.
You cannot speak of ice
to a summer insect,
the creature of a season.

CHUANG TZU

October is the fallen leaf,
but it is also a wider horizon
more clearly seen.
It is the distant hills
once more in sight,
and the enduring constellations
above them once again.

HAL BORLAND

⸺⊱⋆⊰⸺

Always design a thing
by considering it
in its next larger context—
a chair in a room,
a room in a house,
a house in an environment,
an environment
in a city plan.

ELIEL SAARINEN

In great affairs
we ought to apply ourselves
less to creating chances
than to profiting
from those that offer.

FRANÇOIS LA ROCHEFOUCAULD

Visionary people are visionary
partly because of
the very great many things
they don't see.

BERKELEY RICE

Vision is the art
of seeing things invisible.

JONATHAN SWIFT

The fellow that can only see
a week ahead
is always the popular fellow,
for he is looking
with the crowd.
But the one that can see
years ahead,
he has a telescope
but he can't make anybody believe
he has it.

WILL ROGERS

One never notices
what has been done;
one can only see
what remains to be done.

MARIE CURIE

He who can see
three days ahead
will be rich
for three thousand years.

JAPANESE PROVERB

A rock pile
ceases to be a rock pile
the moment a single man
contemplates it,
bearing within him the image
of a cathedral.

ANTOINE DE SAINT-EXUPERY

You can't have a better tomorrow
if you are thinking about yesterday
all the time.

CHARLES F. KETTERING

I'm a joker
who has understood his epoch
and has extracted all
he possibly could
from the stupidity,
greed and vanity
of his contemporaries.

PABLO PICASSO

To see a World in a
Grain of Sand
And a heaven in a
Wild Flower,
Hold Infinity in the
palm of your hand
And Eternity
in an hour.

WILLIAM BLAKE

The world values the seer
above all men,
and has always done so.
Nay, it values all men in proportion
as they partake of the character of seers.
The Elgin Marbles
and a decision of John Marshall
are valued for the same reason.
What we feel in them
is a painstaking submission
to facts beyond the author's control,
and to ideas imposed upon him
by his vision.

JOHN JAY CHAPMAN

Living and dreaming
are two separate things—
but you can't do one
without the other.

MALCOLM FORBES

WEALTH

The belief in the existence
of opportunities
to achieve economic equality
has had a longer
and more vital tradition
in American history
than has been the case
anywhere else.

LOUIS HACKER

Life begets life.
Energy creates energy.
It is only by spending oneself
that one becomes rich.

SARAH BERNHARDT

It requires a great deal of boldness
and a great deal of caution
to make a great fortune,
and when you have got it,
it requires ten times as much wit
to keep it.

RALPH WALDO EMERSON

Old men
are always advising
young men
to save money.
That is bad advice.
Don't save every nickel.
Invest in yourself.
I never saved a dollar
until I was forty years old.

HENRY FORD

If you want to get rich
from writing,
write the sort of thing
that's read by persons
who move their lips
when they're reading
to themselves.

DON MARQUIS

That some should be rich,
shows that others may become rich,
and hence is just encouragement
to industry and enterprise.

ABRAHAM LINCOLN

Money may be
the husk of many things,
but not the kernel.
It brings you food,
but not appetite;
medicine,
but not health;
acquaintances,
but not friends;
servants,
but not faithfulness;
days of joy,
but not peace or happiness.

HENRIK IBSEN

Money is like a sixth sense
without which you cannot make a complete use
of the other five.

SOMERSET MAUGHAM

Just as war is waged
with the blood of others,
fortunes are made
with other people's money.

ANDRÉ SAURES

He is not fit for riches
who is afraid to use them.

THOMAS FULLER

Well, yes,
you could say
we have independent means.

JOHN D. ROCKEFELLER III

The safest way
to double your money
is to fold it over once
and put it in your pocket.

KIN HUBBARD

———❦———

Money doesn't care
who makes it.

OLD RETAIL SAYING

———❦———

There's no reason
to be the richest man
in the cemetery.
You can't do any business
from there.

COLONEL SANDERS

I wish I were
either rich enough
or poor enough
to do a lot of things
that are impossible
in my present
comfortable circumstances.

DON HEROLD

It's easy to be independent
when you've got money.
But to be independent
when you haven't got a thing—
that's the Lord's test.

MAHALIA JACKSON

INDEX